The Seasons

In spring, the gently falling rain,
Makes the earth all green again.
In summer, sun shines on the ground,
And we see flowers all around.
In autumn, winds blow 'round us all,
To make the leaves turn brown and fall.
In winter, snow drifts white and deep,
To make a blanket for earth's sleep.

Gloria T. Delamar

Little People™ Big Book

About
SEASONS

ALEXANDRIA, VIRGINIA

Table of Contents

All Year Long

Spring

Summer

Fall

Winter

All Year Long

The Four Seasons

Summer
The earth is warm, the sun's ablaze,
it is a time of carefree days;
and bees abuzz that chance to pass
may see me snoozing on the grass.

Fall
The leaves are yellow, red, and brown,
a shower sprinkles softly down;
the air is fragrant, crisp, and cool,
and once again I'm stuck in school.

Winter
The birds are gone, the world is white,
the winds are wild, they chill and bite;
the ground is thick with slush and sleet,
and I can barely feel my feet.

Spring
The fields are rich with daffodils,
a coat of clover cloaks the hills,
and I must dance, and I must sing
to see the beauty of the spring.

Jack Prelutsky

REASONS FOR SEASONS

Winter, spring, summer, and fall are the four seasons of the year.
In most places, winter days are short and the sun doesn't climb very high in the sky. So the earth, the air, and the oceans are all cold. Plants rest, and sometimes snow lies on the ground.

Clean, white snow is lots of fun to play with. Can you find the children who are sledding? How about the skaters? Do you see the snowman?

Sometimes animals use the snow to hide. If their fur is white, they blend with the snow. Where are the four white rabbits?

When spring comes, the days begin to get longer. The sun stays longer in the sky, so the earth becomes warmer. Snow begins to melt, which helps water plants. The plants begin to grow. Spring arrives!

Spring is the time when all kinds of baby animals are born. Can you find all the baby animals?

As the earth gets softer, people work in gardens and on farms. Where are they in this picture?

Other people like to spend time by the water. Do you see them here?

9

In summer, days are very long. The earth where you live tilts toward the sun. So the earth is at its warmest. Plants are green and growing. If you go swimming, the water is nice and warm.

A scarecrow helps keep birds away from the summer vegetables as they grow. Can you find the scarecrow?

In the summertime woods, you can sometimes see a deer somewhere in the trees. Can you find the deer? How about three chickens? And where are the ducks?

When fall comes, the days become shorter. The sun isn't as strong in the sky. Fall is the time when plants prepare for their winter sleep once again.

On a bright fall day, the leaves are bright, colorful, and cheery. Look for someone playing in the leaves. Sometimes you'll see a squirrel gathering acorns and nuts for the winter. Where are the squirrels in this picture?

Fall is pumpkin time! Pumpkins grow on vines which lie on the ground. Can you find the pumpkin patch? How about a basket of apples?

13

Spring

Spring

I'm shouting
I'm singing
I'm swinging through trees
I'm winging sky-high
With the buzzing black bees.
I'm the sun
I'm the moon
I'm the dew on the rose.
I'm a rabbit
Whose habit
Is twitching his nose.
I'm lively
I'm lovely
I'm kicking my heels.
I'm crying "Come dance"
to the freshwater eels.
I'm racing through meadows
Without any coat
I'm a gamboling lamb
I'm a light leaping goat
I'm a bud
I'm a bloom
I'm a dove on the wing.
I'm running rooftops
And welcoming spring!

Karla Kuskin

A CLOSER LOOK:
HOW A CHICK IS HATCHED

So much happens inside a little chicken egg!

An egg is made up of the yolk (which is the yellow part), the white, and the shell. A chick needs these parts of the egg to help it grow, but none of these parts is the chick itself.

A chick begins to grow inside its mother, the hen. When the egg is first laid, the chick is just a speck on the yolk. A tube grows from the chick to the yolk. The yolk will feed the chick as it grows. Around the yolk is the thick, gooey egg white. It keeps the chick from getting bumped around. The hard shell holds everything together and protects the chick once the egg comes out of the hen. When it comes out, the egg must stay

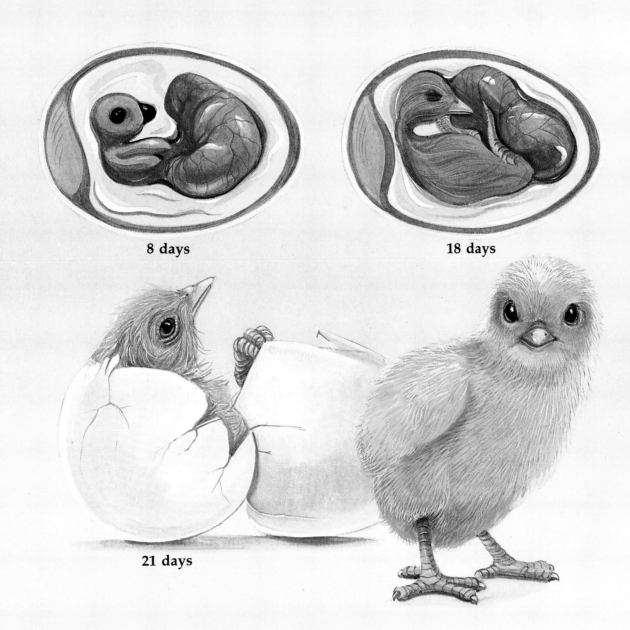

8 days

18 days

21 days

warm so the chick can grow. The hen can sit on the egg and keep it warm under her soft feathers, or the egg can be put into an incubator, a machine that will keep it warm.

It takes three weeks for the chick to grow big enough to come out of the egg. Finally the chick begins to hatch. *Peck, peck, peck!* The chick pecks with its beak to break a hole in the eggshell. Cracking the shell is hard work and takes a long time. *Peck, peck, peck!* At last the chick is hatched! Its feathers are wet. It is too tired to stand up. The chick rests until it can stand on its two little legs. Before long, it is dry and fluffy.

And that is how a chick is hatched.

Splish! Splosh! Splash!

by Michael J. Pellowski

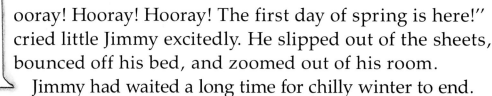

ooray! Hooray! Hooray! The first day of spring is here!" cried little Jimmy excitedly. He slipped out of the sheets, bounced off his bed, and zoomed out of his room.

Jimmy had waited a long time for chilly winter to end. Now, at long last, it was over. Spring had finally arrived.

Spring was Jimmy's favorite season. He liked to play in the bright sunshine. He liked to watch the flowers grow and the grass turn green. Spring was when all the birds returned and chirped merrily. Springtime was *fun* time. Jimmy couldn't wait to go outside and play.

Jimmy zipped into the living room and looked out the window. *Splish! Splosh! Splash!* Big drops of rain splattered against the window-panes. "Oh, no!" Jimmy moaned sadly.

"What's wrong?" Jimmy's mother asked.

"Spring is here," groaned Jimmy. "But it's *raining* outside!"

"Sometimes it rains in spring," Jimmy's mom explained. "Spring rain makes things grow."

"I know," sighed Jimmy. "But spring should be sunny. How can a rainy spring be fun?" He glanced at the window again. *Splish! Splosh! Splash!* Rain gently beat against the pane.

Jimmy's mom smiled. "We'll find a way to make this day fun," she said.

Jimmy slowly went back upstairs to dress.

After breakfast, his mother took him to the coat closet. "Now we'll dress you for your day of fun," she said. She helped Jimmy put on a bright yellow raincoat. She put a matching rain hat with a wide brim on his head. Then she slipped big, floppy galoshes over his shoes. "Now you can go outside and play on this first day of spring," she said.

Out into the rain went Jimmy. *Splatter! Patter! Patter!* The little raindrops beat out a merry tune as they fell on Jimmy's hat and coat. "It sounds just like music," said Jimmy as he started to smile. "The rain is playing a spring song!" he said as he danced up and down the sidewalk.

Out on the grass, robins were busy hunting for food. They had just arrived after a long flight from their winter homes. They began to sing happily. *Chirp! Chirp! Chirp!*

"This is a *wonderful* spring day after all," as he skipped to a big puddle. *SPLISH!* He leaped into the puddle. *SPLOSH!* He hopped toward the other side. *SPLASH!* Out he jumped.

"Hooray!" he cried. "Mom was right! A rainy spring day can be fun!" *Splish! Splosh! Splash!* Jimmy stomped his way through puddles big and small.

20

When Jimmy tired of splashing, he played a new game. He brought out a little boat and floated it in the biggest puddle he could find. "I am the captain of this ship!" Jimmy cried. "And I am sailing through a stormy sea." He pulled the boat back and forth in the water. *Splish! Splosh! Splash!* Down came the rain.

Jimmy was bouncing his boat through the water when he heard his mother. She was calling to him, "Look up!" Jimmy saw a beautiful rainbow in the sky. The sun was about to peek through the clouds. It had stopped raining, and Jimmy hadn't even noticed!

Some of Jimmy's friends had come out and were gathering near a big puddle left by the rain. Jimmy was about to run over to them when his mother called to him again. She asked him to come in and take off his rain clothes.

"It looks like tomorrow is going to be a sunny spring day," she said.

"Oh, no!" sighed Jimmy. "I had so much fun today, I wish it would rain again!"

21

RAINY DAY POEMS

Sun After Rain

Rain, rain,
Went away.
Sun came out
with pipe of clay,
blew a bubble
whole-world-wide,
stuck a rainbow
on one side.

Norma Farber

Raindrops

How brave a ladybug must be!
Each drop of rain is big as she.

Can you imagine what you'd do
If raindrops fell as big as you?

Aileen Fisher

It's Raining! It's Pouring!

It's raining! It's pouring!
The old man is snoring.

He bumped his head and went to bed
And couldn't get up in the morning!

Traditional

23

Snow-White and Rose-Red

A Retelling of the Fairy Tale by the Brothers Grimm

n old woman and her two daughters lived in a little cottage in a great forest. One daughter, Snow-White, had soft, yellow hair, and the other, Rose-Red, was dark with pink cheeks and lips. The sisters kept two rosebushes, one of which bore white flowers and the other red, and they cared well for each other and their good mother.

One winter night, after they had all settled in, there was a knock at the door. "Quick, Snow-White, open the door; it may be a traveler in need," said their mother, and Snow-White obeyed.

Outside the door was a huge black bear, nearly frozen with cold. Snow-White shrieked and Rose-Red trembled, but the bear said, "Do not be afraid! I won't hurt you. But I must warm myself by your fire, if you will allow me."

The mother curtsied and welcomed the bear in. The bear lumbered into the room, groaning because his paws were aching with frost. In no time at all, he fell asleep in the warmth.

The sisters saw how sweet-tempered the bear was, so the following morning, they made him an excellent breakfast. The bear thanked them for their trouble, then padded away into the snow, but he came back that night, and every night for weeks. As time went by, the mother and her daughters grew very fond of him.

But one warm spring morning, the bear told them he would not return until the end of the summer, and they tearfully parted. As Snow-White and Rose-Red watched the bear leave, they saw him catch his fur on one of the rosebushes, and thought they spied a glint of gold underneath it.

Not long after that, the sisters were walking in the woods when they came upon a dwarf. His long white beard was stuck in the cleft of a fallen tree, and he was hopping about like a grasshopper. "Don't be so timid!" the dwarf yelled. "Help me!" Snow-White took a pair of scissors from her apron pocket and carefully snipped off the end of his beard, freeing him.

But was the dwarf grateful? Indeed, he was not! He snarled, "You have cut off a piece of my splendid beard! A pox on you!" And he snatched up a sack of gold that lay hidden in the grass and disappeared in a wink.

Not long after that, Snow-White and Rose-Red came upon the dwarf again, this time by a stream. His white beard was entangled in a fishing line, and an energetic fish was about to tug him into the water. "Help me, and hurry!" he bellowed.

"Hold still," advised Rose-Red, and she snipped off the trapped beard. Again the dwarf bounded free, but this time he was angrier than before. "Doesn't my beautiful beard mean anything to you? You foolish girls!" he shouted. He snatched up a sack of pearls from behind a stone and vanished.

Another day, on their way to the village, the sisters heard a raucous noise and saw a great eagle struggling to carry off the very same dwarf. The sisters rushed to help and managed to catch hold of his arms and legs and tear him from the eagle's grasp, but it was some effort, and in the fight the dwarf's fine clothes became tattered and torn.

"You oafs! Don't you know better than to tear my clothes?" he shouted at them. He grabbed a bag of rubies that lay hidden in the nearby weeds, and dashed into a cave.

On their way back from the village that very evening, Snow-White and Rose-Red again came upon the dwarf. He was sitting in front of his cave, with his treasures spread on the ground before him. They sparkled in the low evening light. The sisters couldn't help but stare at the sight. The dwarf began to yell at them for gawking, when suddenly an enormous black bear arose out of the forest and bore down upon the little group.

"Oh, mercy! Don't hurt me!" begged the dwarf. "If you're hungry, eat those two fine fat girls over there! They're wicked creatures, and the world would be well rid of them!"

But the bear knocked the dwarf over with his mighty paw, and that was the end of the dwarf.

Snow-White and Rose-Red trembled in terror before the bear, but the creature's fur coat suddenly fell away. Standing before them was a handsome young man, who smiled and said, "I am a Prince. That evil dwarf stole my treasures and cast a spell on me. Only his death could set me free. But because you two were kind to me when I was a bear, I will share my treasures with you."

And he did. The Prince married Snow-White, and his brother married Rose-Red. They all lived together happily in a palace with the sisters' mother. And outside the palace they planted two rosebushes—one white and one red.

Summer

Barefoot Days

In the morning, very early,
That's the time I love to go
Barefoot where the fern grows curly
And grass is cool between each toe,
On a summer morning—O!
On a summer morning!

That is when the birds go by
Up the sunny slopes of air,
And each rose has a butterfly
Or a golden bee to wear;
And I am glad in every toe—
Such a summer morning—O!
Such a summer morning!

Rachel Field

DID YOU EVER WONDER
ABOUT THE SUN

What is the sun?
The sun is really a star, just like the stars you see in the sky at night. But the sun is much closer to the earth than any other star, so it looks much bigger and much brighter. Our planet, Earth, travels through space in a giant circle around the sun. So do Mercury, Venus, and all the other planets.

What is the sun made of?
If you could travel to the sun, there would be no place to stand, because the sun is not solid like the earth. The sun is a great ball of gas. The sun is also very, very hot, much hotter than any fire or furnace. The sun is so hot that we feel its heat here on earth, millions of miles away.

Why does the sun move across the sky?

It looks as though the sun travels across the sky every day, rising in the east and setting in the west. But the sun only seems to move in the sky because the earth is turning. When the part of the earth where you live turns toward the sun, it is daytime. When your part of the earth turns away from the sun, it is night. Whenever it is daytime in one part of the world, it is nighttime somewhere else.

What causes sunburn?

Along with heat and light, other types of energy come from the sun. Our bodies need some of this energy, but too much can be harmful. When you get a painful sunburn, it's your body's way of saying you've been out in the sun too long. That's why it's a good idea to protect your skin with clothing or a sun block if you're going to be outside for a long time on a sunny day.

The Tale of Peter Rabbit

An Adaptation of the Story by Beatrix Potter

Once upon a time there were four little rabbits, and their names were Flopsy, Mopsy, Cottontail, and Peter. They lived underneath the root of a very big fir tree.

"Now, my dears," said old Mrs. Rabbit one morning, "you may go into the fields or down the lane, but don't go into Mr. McGregor's garden. Your father had an accident there; he was put in a pie by Mrs. McGregor."

Then old Mrs. Rabbit took a basket and her umbrella and went through the wood to the baker's. She bought a loaf of brown bread and five currant buns.

Flopsy, Mopsy, and Cottontail, who were good little bunnies, went down the lane to gather blackberries. But Peter, who was very naughty, ran straight away to Mr. McGregor's garden and squeezed under the gate!

First he ate some lettuce and some French beans, and then he ate some radishes. And then, feeling rather sick, he went to look for some parsley. But, 'round the end of a cucumber frame, whom should he meet but Mr. McGregor!

Mr. McGregor was on his hands and knees planting out young cabbages, but he jumped up and ran after Peter, waving a rake and calling out, "Stop, thief!"

Peter was most dreadfully frightened; he rushed all over the garden, for he had forgotten the way back to the gate. He lost one of his shoes among the cabbages, and the other shoe among the potatoes. After losing them, he ran on four legs and went faster, so that he might have gotten away altogether if he had not unfortunately run into a gooseberry net and got caught by the large buttons on his jacket. It was a blue jacket with brass buttons, quite new.

Peter gave himself up for lost, and shed big tears; but his sobs were overheard by some friendly sparrows, who flew to him in great excitement, and implored him to exert himself.

Mr. McGregor came up with a sieve, which he intended to pop upon the top of Peter; but Peter wriggled out just in time, leaving his jacket behind him. Then he rushed into the tool shed and jumped into a can. It would have been a wonderful thing to hide in, if it had not had so much water in it.

Mr. McGregor was quite sure that Peter was somewhere in the tool shed, perhaps hidden underneath a flowerpot. He began to turn them over carefully, looking under each.

Presently Peter sneezed—"Kertyschoo!" Mr. McGregor was after him in no time, and tried to put his foot upon Peter, who jumped out of a window, upsetting three plants. The window was too small for Mr. McGregor, and he was tired of running after Peter. He went back to his work.

Peter sat down to rest; he was out of breath and trembling with fright, and he had not the least idea which way to go. Also, he was very damp from sitting in that can.

After a time he began to wander about, going lippity, lippity—not very fast—and looking all around. He had to find the gate so he could get out of the garden! Suddenly, quite close to him, he heard the noise of a hoe—*scr-r-ritch, scratch, scratch, scritch*. Peter saw Mr. McGregor hoeing onions. His back was turned toward Peter, and beyond him was the gate!

Peter started running as fast as he could go, along a straight walk behind some black currant bushes. Mr. McGregor caught sight of him at the corner, but Peter did not care. He slipped underneath the gate, and was safe at last in the wood outside the garden.

Mr. McGregor hung up the little jacket and the shoes for a scarecrow to frighten the blackbirds.

Peter never stopped running or looked behind him until he got home to the big fir tree. He was so tired that he flopped down upon the nice soft sand on the floor of the rabbit hole and shut his eyes. His mother was busy cooking; she wondered what he had done with his clothes. It was the second little jacket and pair of shoes that Peter had lost in two weeks!

Peter was not very well during that evening. His mother put him to bed and made some camomile tea, and she gave a dose of it to Peter: "One tablespoonful to be taken at bedtime."

But Flopsy, Mopsy, and Cottontail had bread and milk and blackberries for supper!

A CLOSER LOOK:
BUTTERFLIES

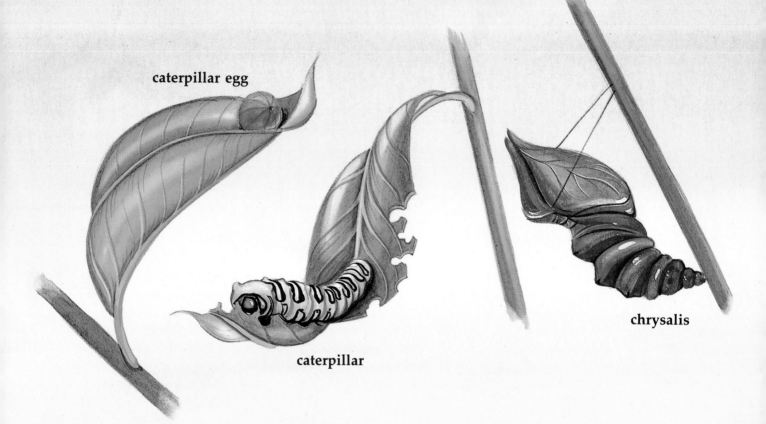

caterpillar egg

caterpillar

chrysalis

Have you ever watched colorful butterflies flying about in the summer? Each one was once a fuzzy little caterpillar that began its life in an egg. Once it hatches from the egg, the caterpillar does nothing but eat. Often, one of the first things it eats is its own eggshell! It eats fruits and leaves to help it grow bigger. As it grows, it keeps outgrowing its skin, so it sheds the skin many times. Each time, there's a new, baggy skin underneath.

When the caterpillar is finished growing, it finds a good place to hibernate, or take a long, long rest. It attaches itself to a twig or the underside of a leaf. The caterpillar then sheds its skin one last time. Underneath its skin is a shell, or chrysalis, that will soon harden.

   Some caterpillars will stay inside this shell for only ten days; others will stay inside for months. The shell hangs still. From the outside, it looks as if nothing is happening. But inside, many changes are taking place. Just before the creature comes out of its shell, its wings gain color. Its body cracks the shell open and a butterfly appears! After about half an hour, the butterfly begins to fly.

   A butterfly can't bite or chew. It uses its jaws to form tubes that help it suck nectar from flowers. It uses its antennae to feel and smell things. And even though a butterfly has six legs, the legs aren't strong and the butterfly can't walk far on them. Flying is the best way to get around!

IT'S SUMMERTIME!

It's summertime! Let's have some fun.
We'll have a picnic in the sun.

We'll chase a butterfly through the fields
And ride a bike with just two wheels!

Roast some marshmallows over a fire,
Watch a kite fly higher and higher,

Have a cookout under the sky
And watch our friends go skating by.

We'll swing on the swings, read under a tree,
Play baseball, eat hot dogs, and drink some iced tea.

We'll swim in the water and lie on a float,
Sail with the breeze on a lake in a boat!

We'll build a tree house all our own,
Eat corn on the cob and an ice cream cone,

Dig in the sand, play tag, and camp out—
This is what summer is all about!

Can you find all the summertime activities on these pages?

Fall

Fall

The last of October
We lock the garden gate.
The flowers have all withered
That used to stand straight.

The last of October
We put the swings away
And the porch looks deserted
Where we like to play.

The last of October
The birds have all flown,
The screens are in the attic,
The sandpile's alone:

Everything is put away
Before it starts to snow—
I wonder if the ladybugs
Have any place to go!

Aileen Fisher

A CLOSER LOOK:
LEAVES

Look up at a tree on a beautiful fall day and you will probably see orange, or red, or yellow leaves. Or maybe you'll see brown, or pink, or even purple!

Why don't leaves stay green? Each leaf has many colors in it. During the spring and summer, leaves are green because they are filled with chlorophyll. Chlorophyll is green, and it hides the other colors in the leaf.

Leaves catch sunshine, and chlorophyll turns the sunshine into food for the tree. But then fall comes. The weather gets colder and the days get shorter. Just as some animals hibernate during the winter, some trees spend the coldest part of the year "asleep." They don't need much food while they're sleeping. So the leaves don't need to catch sunshine for them. The chlorophyll in the leaves begins to disappear. Then the other colors in the leaves—red, yellow, orange—show up, because the chlorophyll isn't there to hide them anymore. Soon after, the leaves fall off the trees.

But soon spring comes, the trees wake up, and it all happens again!

FIVE RED APPLES

Fall is the time when apples ripen and fall off the tree.
In this fingerplay you can pretend your fingers are apples.

Five red apples hanging in a tree,
The juiciest apples you ever did see.
The wind came by and gave an angry frown,
And one little apple came tumbling down.

Four red apples hanging in a tree,
The juiciest apples you ever did see.
The wind came by and gave an angry frown,
And one little apple came tumbling down.

Keep repeating the fingerplay until all the "apples"
are gone.

1. Five red apples hanging
in a tree . . .
(Hold up hand, palm out,
fingers extended.)

2. The juiciest apples you ever
did see . . .
(Wiggle fingers.)

3. The wind came by and gave
an angry frown . . .
(Move index fingers across lips
and pull lips down to form a frown.)

4. And one little apple came
tumbling down.
(Hold up hand, palm out,
fingers extended. Then tuck
thumb into palm.)

Johnny Appleseed
A Retelling of an American Folktale

 long time ago, when America was still a very young country, there was a man who loved apples. His name was John Chapman.

John set out to plant apple trees for the settlers who were going west to raise their families. He liked to tell his friends, the Indians, "I'm going to plant apple orchards in every corner of this land!" He carried a leather pouch filled with apple seeds, and wore a hat stuck with feathers from the birds who fed from his hand. Everyone he met liked him for his warmth and kindness, and he was soon known as Johnny Appleseed.

One spring, during his travels, Johnny met up with a band of woodsmen. "We can arm wrestle with the toughest grizzly bears," they boasted. Then they challenged Johnny to a wrestling match.

"I've got a better idea," said Johnny. "How about a tree-chopping race?"

The woodsmen eagerly agreed. But by the end of the day, all the woodsmen were stretched out on the ground, exhausted, while Johnny stood tall.

"Thanks for your help, boys!" said Johnny, looking around at the fallen trees. "This is a good spot for a new apple orchard, now that you've helped me clear it!"

Johnny continued hiking all over the west, planting his apple seeds and watching them grow. Along the way, he helped settlers raise their barns, and entertained their children with stories of his adventures. He told them about how he slept in a hollowed-out log during a terrible storm, and how he once was bitten by a rattlesnake on the bottom of his foot. Fortunately for him, his feet were as tough as rawhide from all his walking.

When he grew older, he had long white hair. He wore an old mush pan turned upside down as a hat. It made a wonderful roof when it rained, and he carried it along with his sack of seeds. His clothes were tattered. His feet were bare. But he still kept traveling and planting apple orchards, sometimes returning to trim and care for the young trees as they grew.

Many of those apple trees still stand. And every fall, Johnny Appleseed presents us with a gift of apples. We make warm apple pies, and tangy cider, and delicious applesauce from them. Next time you bite into an apple, think of Johnny Appleseed.

The Dark, Dark House

In the dark, dark wood there was
   a dark, dark house,
And in that dark, dark house, there was
   a dark, dark room,
And in that dark, dark room, there was
   a dark, dark cupboard,
And in that dark, dark cupboard, there was
   a dark, dark shelf,
And on that dark, dark shelf, there was
   a dark, dark box,
And in that dark, dark box, there was a . . .

GHOST!

Traditional

51

Over the River and Through the Woods

Over the river and through the woods,
To Grandmother's house we go;
The horse knows the way to carry the sleigh
Through the white and drifted snow.

Over the river and through the woods,
Oh, how the wind does blow!
It stings the toes and bites the nose,
As over the ground we go.

Over the river and through the woods,
Trot fast, my dapple gray!
Spring over the ground like a hunting hound,
For this is Thanksgiving Day.

Over the river and through the woods,
Now Grandfather's face I spy!
Hurrah for the fun! Is the turkey done?
Hurrah for the pumpkin pie!

Traditional

Winter

My Mother's Got Me Bundled Up

My mother's got me bundled up
in tons of winter clothes,
you could not recognize me
if I did not have a nose.
I'd wear much less, but she'd get mad
if I dared disobey her,
so I stay wrapped from head to toe
in layer after layer.

I am wearing extra sweaters,
I am wearing extra socks,
my galoshes are so heavy
that my ankles seem like rocks.
I am wearing scarves and earmuffs,
I am wearing itchy pants,
my legs feel like they're swarming
with a million tiny ants.

My mittens are enormous
and my coat weighs more than me,
my woolen hat and ski mask
make it difficult to see.
It's hard to move, and when I try
I waddle, then I flop,
I'm the living, breathing model
of a walking clothing shop.

Jack Prelutsky

TRACKS IN THE SNOW

This was a mouse who played around
All by himself one night,
Dancing under the winter moon
Forward and left and right.

This was a pheasant walking by,
Out with a friend or two—
This was a rabbit running fast,
The way rabbits do.

This was a squirrel who found a nut—
This was a chickadee—
And this uncommon sort of track
I think was probably me.

Marchette Chute

Tracks in the snow are like clues to a mystery. Can you find the rabbit's tracks? How about the dancing mouse's?

A CLOSER LOOK:
SNOWFLAKES

Snow is lots of fun to play in—you can throw snowballs, build a snow fort, or decorate a snowman.

Snow is made of tiny ice crystals. These crystals are not frozen raindrops. Instead, droplets of water vapor, which you can't even see in the air, freeze and turn into crystals. When the crystals bump and stick together, they form snowflakes. Sometimes dozens of ice crystals join to make one very large snowflake.

Snow crystals grow in several different shapes. They can look like round plates, or pointy stars. But whether a snowflake is big or small, each one is always flat and has six sides or six points. Yet no two snowflakes are exactly alike.

Snow is filled with air, which makes it light. A blanket of snow can protect plants and hibernating animals from the cold winter. The snow keeps warm air from escaping as it rises up from the ground. Melting snow becomes water for streams and reservoirs.

What's *your* favorite way to play in the snow?

The Snowflake Ballet

One cold winter day,
when the sky was as soft as feathers
and the clouds looked like great gray pillows,
a lonely little snowflake fell
swirling and twirling out of the sky.
Around and around and around it danced
until finally it settled softly
on the big brown nose of a sleepy brown bear.
   Sniff, sniff, went the bear.
He opened his eyes and lifted his nose toward the sky.
"Smells like snow," said the bear. "Hmmm."
And he snuggled deeper into the small cave he called home,
warm and cozy in his thick fur coat.

High up above
on the bare branches of a tall beech tree,
two fat white owls sat watching with their wide, golden eyes.
One blinked once,
the other blinked twice,
and a handful of fluttering flakes slowly spun down and around
and around and down...
to a bed of crackly dry leaves on the ground.
   Three hungry squirrels stopped their chattering
and held their acorns still in their tiny pink paws.
"Snow!" they whispered.
"Snow!" mumbled four chubby chipmunks.
Their cheeks were stuffed with stolen acorns.
"Thieves!" cried the squirrels.
The chipmunks ran.
The squirrels ran.
And the snow came down and down.

61

Five furry foxes huddled in their den,
shivering to the tips of their long, silvery tails.
"Brrr," said the foxes as the snow blew in.
They cuddled close and were warm again.

"Caw, caw, caw, caw, caw, caw," called six inky black crows
from the treetops.
"Snow, snow, snow, snow, snow, SNOW!" they screamed and
flapped as their wings turned frosty white.

The snow whirled and whipped in blustery gusts.
Seven little rabbits hippety-hopped home,
shaking their snowy, wet paws.

On a rocky ledge,
eight shaggy coyotes stood and howled, S N O W—Oooooo!
while in the meadow down below,
nine nimble deer
pranced and danced a snowflake ballet.

62

And as the ground was covered with white,
Mother Mouse kissed her ten tiny babies good night
in a nest of sweet smelling leaves and dried brown grass
and sang a lullaby as soft as the snow.
Hush-a-bye,
hush-a-bye,
sleepy soft snow.
Hush-a-bye, babies,
to dreamland you go.

Stephanie St. Pierre

63

Little People™ Big Book About SEASONS

TIME-LIFE for CHILDREN™

Publisher: Robert H. Smith
Managing Editor: Neil Kagan
Associate Editors: Jean Burke Crawford,
Patricia Daniels
Marketing Director: Ruth P. Stevens
Promotion Director: Kathleen B. Tresnak
Associate Promotion Director: Jane B. Welihozkiy
Production Manager: Prudence G. Harris
Editorial Consultants: Jacqueline A. Ball,
Sara Mark

PRODUCED BY PARACHUTE PRESS, INC.

Editorial Director: Joan Waricha
Editors: Christopher Medina, Jane Stine
Writers: Richard Chevat, Joan Israel,
Gregory Maguire, Michael Pellowski,
Stephanie St. Pierre
Designer: Deborah Michel
Illustrators: Stephanie Britt, Pat and Robin
DeWitt, Jeff DiNardo, Heather King,
Hilary Knight, Turi Macombie,
John Speirs, Linda Weller

Time-Life Books Inc. offers a wide range of fine publications, including home video products. For subscription information, call 1-800-621-7026 or write TIME-LIFE BOOKS, P.O. Box C-32068, Richmond, Virginia 23261-2068.

ACKNOWLEDGMENTS

Every effort has been made to trace the ownership of all copyrighted material and to secure the necessary permissions to reprint these selections. If any question arises as to the use of any material, the editor and the publisher, while expressing regret for any inadvertent error, will make the necessary correction in future printings.

Grateful acknowledgment is made to the following for permission to reprint the copyrighted material listed below: Doubleday, a division of Bantam, Doubleday, Dell Publishing Group, Inc. for "Barefoot Days" from TAXIS AND TOADSTOOLS by Rachael Field. Copyright © 1926 by Doubleday. Aileen Fisher for "Fall". Copyright © 1953 by Aileen Fisher. Greenwillow Books (a division of William Morrow & Co. Inc.) for "My Mother's Got Me Bundled Up" from IT'S SNOWING, IT'S SNOWING by Jack Prelutsky. Copyright © 1984 by Jack Prelutsky. Harper & Row for "Raindrops" from OUT IN THE DARK AND DAYLIGHT by Aileen Fisher. Copyright © 1966 by Aileen Fisher; and "Spring" from DOGS AND DRAGONS, TREES AND DREAMS by Karla Kuskin. Copyright © 1964 by Karla Kuskin. McFarland & Company, Inc. for "The Seasons" from CHILDREN'S COUNTING-OUT RHYMES, FINGERPLAYS, JUMP ROPE AND BOUNCE-BALL CHANTS AND OTHER RHYMES by Gloria T. Delamar. Copyright © 1983 by Gloria T. Delamar. Putnam Publishing Group for "Sun After Rain" from SMALL WONDERS by Norma Farber. Copyright © 1964, 1968, 1969 by Norma Farber. Reprinted by permission of Coward, McCann & Geoghegan. Random House, Inc. for "The Four Seasons" by Jack Prelutsky from THE RANDOM HOUSE BOOK OF POETRY FOR CHILDREN, selected and introduced by Jack Prelutsky. Copyright © 1983 by Random House, Inc. Mary Chute Smith for "Tracks in the Snow" from AROUND AND ABOUT by Marchette Chute. Copyright © 1957 by E.P. Dutton, Inc., renewed 1985 by Marchette Chute.

Library of Congress Cataloging-in-Publication Data

Little people big book about seasons.
    p   cm.
    Summary: A collection of original stories, folktales, essays, poems, activities, and games, about the seasons.
    ISBN 0-8094-7470-0.—ISBN 0-8094-7471-9 (lib. bdg.)
    1. Seasons—Literary collections. [1. Seasons—Literary collections.] I. Time-Life for Children (Firm)
PZ5.L72585 1989
    808.8'033—dc20   89-37468
                                                        CIP
                                                        AC

TIME-LIFE BOOKS
ALEXANDRIA, VIRGINIA

The Seasons

In spring, the gently falling rain,
Makes the earth all green again.
In summer, sun shines on the ground,
And we see flowers all around.
In autumn, winds blow 'round us all,
To make the leaves turn brown and fall.
In winter, snow drifts white and deep,
To make a blanket for earth's sleep.

                                Gloria T. Delamar